The Plays of Faith

Joyce Lee

Order this book online at www.trafford.com
or email orders@trafford.com

Most Trafford titles are also available at major online book retailers.

Printed in the United States of America.

ISBN: 978-1-4669-0930-4 (sc)
ISBN: 978-1-4669-0931-1 (e)

Trafford rev. 12/19/2011

www.trafford.com

North America & international
toll-free: 1 888 232 4444 (USA & Canada)
phone: 250 383 6864 • fax: 812 355 4082

DEDICATION

What a blessing to dedicate this book to my loving husband, Leroy Lee and my two beautiful girls along with their husbands, Tusha Lee Talley(Mark) and Francesca Lee Coleman(David). I would also like to dedicate this book to my precious grandchildren-Dejerra Symone Pradia, Josiah Dewayne Pradia, David Lamar Green, Jazell Elizabeth Coleman and Daydren Mauryon Coleman.

ACKNOWLEDGMENTS

First off let me thank God, for answering my prayers and fulfilling my visions as an author. It was God all by himself that anointed my spirit in this capacity. It is with great gratitude that I give him all the glory and praise for all of his marvelous works.

I can't thank my friends and family enough for supporting my vision. It was their love and support that encouraged me to complete this book. Indeed it took some time to get this book published and finished but I believe through the grace of God all things are possible through him.

To Sister Gloria Lawson: You have been a friend to the end. Whatever I needed, you were there. Your love for me and my vision was unconditional. All I can say is that I know I can depend on you for anything. Thank you again for editing this book and for being so patient and caring with your love and understanding, while I was preparing this book of plays. Thank you.

To Sister Annette Guillory Wallace: You are so awesome and worthy to be praised. God has gifted you with many talents and I can truly say you have been a blessing to me. He has blessed you to be the writer of such a profound play *"Be Careful What You Say-Watch Your Tongue."* This was a vision God gave me and due to my husband illness you were able to complete it. Thank you so very much.

Joyce Lee

To Sister Ruth Johnson: Thank you for helping me direct the play, *Heaven & Hell Wedding*. You're the type of person that everyone need in their lives. May God continue to shower you with many great things.

To Sister Constance Pickens—Burnside: Thank you for showing me information to help me get this book published. Who can find a better person that can tell you straight forward; to keep on keeping on. **P.U.S.H., Push Until Something Happen.**

To Sister Jeanette and Brittany Arceneaux: Thanks for all your effort and time that you sacrificed to make this vision a reality for all to read and joy. I dearly love the both of you.

Last but not least I'd like to thank all of my sisters and brothers in Christ who participated, viewed and supported each one of these plays. Without you it would not have been a blessing to all. I pray that you enjoy.

ACKNOWLEDGEMENTS
Pastor Gregory and Sister Yvette Hunter

We acknowledge and honor our Pastor (The Rev. Gregory Hunter Sr.), for the great job and work he is doing. We appreciate your love and concern for God, his word and his people. So, be encouraged. God really has smiled on you!

We also honor our First Lady (Sister Yvette Hunter), and we say to her, "Favor is deceitful, and beauty is vain, but a woman that fears the Lord, shall be praised".

We truly thank God for the both of you. May God continue to bless you as the Pastor and may all be blessed richly is our prayers.

Sis Joyce Lee

Joyce Lee is a native Houstonian graduating from Evan E. Worthing Sr. High School. She is the president of the Usher & Nurse's Ministry, a Sunday School Teacher and a active member of the Pastor Aide, Mission, Benevolence and Prayer Team at the Starlight Missionary Baptist Church under the leadership of the late Pastor Allen T. Guillory Sr. Also she is a Teacher and Vice-President of the Ark of Love Association Usher and Nurses under the leadership of Moderator E. L. Burnside of Mt. Carmel M. B. C.

For many years Joyce has loved to present programs and plays for the Church or Pastor and Wife Anniversary. In 2008 God inspired her to write her first play *Heaven and Hell Wedding,* which she put on in 2009. God continues to get His message to His people by using her talents. In 2010 God gave her a title of a play *Be Careful What You say (Watch Your Tongue).* She shared her divine inspiration for this play with Sis Annette Guillory-Wallace, who God has used through the Holy Spirit, to write and direct this play. These plays are paving the way for her to share what God has given her.

INTRODUCTION

First, I would like to thank God for all my blessings. In 2007, the Lord gave me a vision to write gospel plays. My main objective is to let people in the world know that it is a reality in serving an all wise God. These plays are based on daily living. It also displays how everyday situations can turn our world upside down. This realization allows you to know that God can fix every circumstance we often find ourselves in. My prayer is that this book will be a blessing to the viewing audience.

Joyce Lee

In Honor of
Our
First Woman of God, Sis P. Guillory
And
The Late Pastor Allen T. Guillory Sr.

The pastor lasting contribution to the Kingdom of God is determined, not by what he thinks, nor by what he preaches, but what he is! A true shepherd gathers, leads, and feeds with sound doctrine, watches over, and in every way endeavors to promote the health, safety, growth, comfort and spiritual life of his people. Therefore he seeks not great things for himself but for the flock in which he oversees.

We as a body of baptized believers have been given a leader and a shepherd that truly has a heart of God and a love for God's people. We truly understand his calling and will follow him as he follows Christ. He and the First Woman of God labor in the vineyard tirelessly to serve the people of God so that all may be saved and none are lost. They are the people that live what they teach.

THE REVELATION OF THE
OLD SHIP OF ZION
INTRODUCTION

The Holy Spirit has bestowed upon Mrs. Joyce H. Lee a phenomenal play "Do the Right Thing to Get on the Ship." Revelation 22:14 says: Blessed are they that do his commandment that they may have a right to the tree of life and may enter in through the gates into the city.

This familiar song lyrics rings out these words to the listening ear-"Tis the old ship of zion, Tis the old ship of zion – get on board. It has landed many a thousands for those who have done the right thing to get on board.

Oh yes, the passengers aboard are young children, young and old adults. Remember, if you don't live right, you will not be able to get on board. Keep in mind when the Lord calls your name we pray that you are doing the right thing. The Lord is coming back and at that point you will know your destination-heaven or hell. This is why we must be about our Father's business. We must do the things that please our Lord and Savior Jesus Christ. We often think it's about us, but it's about God's people. It's about people loving, caring and showing concern for others.

It doesn't matter if you are a minister, missionary, choir member, usher or just a bench member. Mis-treatment of God's people inside or outside the church will cause you to go straight to hell. We must be taught how to do the right thing.

The question was asked, "How can I make it to heaven?"

First, you must be born again!

Secondly, you must get under good leadership which includes biblical teaching and preaching of the word of God.

Third, you must repent. You must turn completely away from sin, and never go that way again.

Finally, you must live the life of a Christian. It must be upheld daily in order to do the right thing to get on the ship.

Now let's reflect back on our love ones who have gone on before us.

THE REVELATION OF THE OLD SHIP OF ZION

Do the Right Thing to get on The Ship
Revelation 22:14
(The Beginning)

Play additions: Props-ship designer-Jesus character-angels (2)-devil character-innkeepers(2)-crowd(several people)-head piece designer

Characters:

Narrator Soloist (2) Duet Singers (2) Ship Carriers (2)

(Soloist stands at designated point on stage)
(Soloist begins singing selected song: Tis the Old Ship of Zion)
(Ship carriers enter carrying the ship – 6 chairs should be behind ship)
(Soloist sings—after each scene)
(Appointed duet perform their song at this time)

(Each scene is acted out after the Narrator reads the scripture or introduces the scene)

Scene I
St. Mark 2:1-12
(The Hole in the Roof)

Characters: Friend (4) – the man with palsy-the scribe –soloist

(4 friends & man with palsy get on ship)

Narrator: And when he returned to Caper'na-um after some days, it was reported that he was at home. And many were gathered together, so that there was no longer room for them, not even about the door; and he was preaching the word to them. And they came, bringing to him a paralytic carried by four men. And when they could not get near him because of the crowd, they removed the roof above him; and when they had made an opening, they let down the pallet on which the paralytic lay. And when Jesus saw their faith , he said to the paralytic, "My son, your sins are forgiven." Now some of the scribes were sitting there, questioning in their hearts, "Why does this man speak thus? It is blasphemy! Who can forgive sins but God alone? And immediately Jesus, perceiving in his spirit that they thus questioned within themselves, said to them, "Why do you question thus in your hearts? Which is easier to say to the paralytic, 'Your sins are forgiven,' or to say, 'Rise, take up your pallet and walk'? But that you may know that the Son of man has authority on earth to forgive sins"—he said to the paralytic—I say to you, rise, take up your pallet and go home." And he rose, and immediately took up the pallet and went out before them all; so that they were all amazed and glorified God, saying " We never saw anything like this!"

Scene II
St. Luke 10:25-37
(The Good Samaritan)

Characters: Narrator-robber-priest-certain man—the Levite-a good Samaritan-coming home (Soloist)

(Good Samaritan gets on ship)

Narrator: And behold, a certain lawyer stood up, and tempted him, saying, Master, what shall I do to inherit eternal life? He said unto him, What is written in the law? How readest thou? And he answering said, Thou shall love the Lord thy God with all thy heart, and with all thy soul, and with all thy strength, and with all thy mind; and thy neighbor as thyself. And he said unto him, Thou hast answered right: this do, and thou shalt live. But he, willing to justify himself, said unto Jesus, and who is my neighbor? And Jesus answering said, A certain man went down from Jerusalem to Jericho, and fell among thieves, which stripped him of his raiment, and wounded him, and departed, leaving him half dead. And by chance there came down a certain priest that way: and when he saw him, he passed by on the other side. And likewise a Levite, when he was at the place, came and looked on him, and passed by on the other side. But a certain Samaritan, as he journeyed, came where he was: and when he saw him, he had compassion on him. And went to him, and bound up his wounds, pouring on oil and wine, and set him on his own beast, and brought him to an inn and took care of him. And on the morrow when he departed, he took out two pence, and gave them to the host, and said unto him, Take care of him; and whatsoever thou spendest more, when I come again, I will repay thee. Which now of these three, thinkest thou, was neighbor unto him that fell among the thieves? And he said, He that showed mercy in him. Then said Jesus unto him, Go, and do thou likewise.

Finale
(The Prodigal Son Coming Home)

Characters: the prodigal son – father—brother –soloist)

(Prodigal son gets on ship)

Narrator: Who is the father of this prodigal son? Who is the brother of this prodigal son? Who could this possible be? He had spent all of his possessions. He has found himself in the lowest place—the hog pen. But oh, when he came to himself, when he realized where he was, what he was surrounded by, it was then he decided to go home. With a sincere heart he asked God first to forgive him. I believe when he arrived home he asked his earthly Father to forgive him too. The **Prodigal Son** did " **THE RIGHT THING TO GET ON THE SHIP."**

A Heaven and Hell Wedding

This vision is based on Godly and un-Godly living. Titus 2:12
This is what our First Woman of God and our late Pastor have
taught us.
This play is in honor to let them know that their preaching and
teaching is not in vain.
Truly, the word of God was exemplified in our late pastor's life and
is still being epitomized in our First Woman of God.
So watch God through the Holy Spirit as he manifests his
awesome powers through this play.

A Heaven and Hell Wedding
Introduction

First, let's take an inventory of heaven. Heaven is a spiritual state of everlasting communion with God: a place of supreme happiness; an abode of blissful spiritual life after death; also, a holy dwelling place for people that are living Godly lives.

Psalm 4:3 says "But know that the Lord hath set apart him that is Godly for himself: the Lord will hear when I call unto him." When we live Godly lives, men will see our good works and glorify our Father, which is in Heaven .

Second, let's take an inventory of hell. Hell is the realm of the devil in which the damned suffer everlasting punishment; a place or state of torment or destruction.

When we live ungodly lives and don't really try to live right, we will go to hell. God knows and reads the heart of men. God is the judge of all—which means everyone. 2 Peter 2:4 says "For if God spared not the angels that sinned, but cast them down to hell, and delivered them into the chains of darkness to be reserved unto judgment.

(PAUSE)

As you look and listen to this play, you can also take inventory of your life. Are you taking a stand for JESUS? or Are you taking a stand for the devil? . . . .

God created the world and he included us. At first everything was good-exactly as God made it! Some of us have made bad decisions and committed wrong actions. Some of us fail to live godly lives and so we become guilty of sin. Our sin separates us from God. So when we sin, we must pray and ask for forgiveness. 1 John 1:9 says "If we confess our sins, he is faithful and just to forgive us our sins, and to cleanse us from all unrighteousness." The only way to God is through Jesus Christ. When God's son came to earth to die on the cross, he took the punishment for our sins. At this point Jesus became the way between God, the Father and us.

(PAUSE)

Sometimes we go contrary to the word of God. Sometimes things just happen and we recognize that it was nobody but God who brought us out and through our troubles. There are those who will not recognize that it was God because of their ungodly living.

John 3:16 says, "For God so loved the world that he gave his only begotten son (Jesus) that whosoever believeth in him should not perish, but have everlasting life. It doesn't matter how young or how old you are—if you are living an ungodly life; don't change and don't call on Jesus—you will not enter into the kingdom of Heaven.

It doesn't matter if you can preach, teach or speak well.

It doesn't matter if you tithe or give an offering.

It doesn't matter if you are the loudest amen member in the church.

It doesn't matter if you wear the finest clothes.

It doesn't matter how well you pray.

It doesn't matter if you do wrong. (Jesus will help you.)

It doesn't matter if you have cussed somebody.

It doesn't matter if you get sick and have a heart attack.

It doesn't matter if you have wrong thoughts in your mind.

It doesn't matter if you have stolen from the one who helps you.

It doesn't matter if you have talked down somebody.

It doesn't matter if you have done drugs. (repent or witness)

It doesn't matter if you've been drinking.

If you want to change your way of living, call upon the Lord Jesus Christ. He is faithful and just to forgive your sins.

Now determine where you want to spend eternity . . . . Will it be heaven or hell?

Only you can answer that question.

There will be some people that will go straight to hell. They love living ungodly, believing that it is not necessary to confess or repent of their sins. And there were some people that were on their way to hell, but repented at the end and went to heaven. There were others that thought that they were going to heaven, because they lead songs in the choir, dressed up to be seen, paid large tithes,and went to church all the time. But at the end, they went to hell.

Scene I
(Hell)

Characters: Bridesmaid 1—bridesmaid 2—bridesmaid 3-Groomsmen 1-groomsmen 2—groomsmen 3—Jesus-flower girl—ring bearer—hell bride

(Each Bridesmaid and Groomsmen walk down aisle together. They stop when they reach Jesus)

Bridesmaid 1—I've come to Rock Hill Missionary Baptist Church right before the message, so I can walk down the aisle. You see, I can draw attention to myself with my tough Liz Claibourne leather suit with matching gloves, hat, purse and shoes on. It's about me and nobody else! People always tell me, "Girl you sho look good."

Groomsmen 1 – Now you already know I have to be seen too. I'm a preacher, when their eyes hit the pulpit, all the attention will be on me. I got on my Steve Harvey with my matching shirt, tie and hat. When I do my holy dance, they will see my Stacy Adams shoes, and everything else I got on. Can't nobody touch this!

Bridesmaid 1 – You're right, I'm sure we will be the best dressed saints heaven has ever seen!

Jesus – You pretend to be a soldier in God's army, but you are really wolves in sheep clothing. You are occasional dressers. Esphesians 6:11-37 says: "We must put on our armor daily to stand against the devil . Stand firm with the belt of truth, the breastplate of righteousness. Fix your feet with the gospel of peace, using the shield of faith, the helmet of salvation and the sword of the spirit which is the word of God." The armor you put on looks good, but it wasn't effective. Therefore you are a casualty of war. Depart from me, you workers of iniquity!

Bridesmaid 2 – I'm trying to get to heaven, so I'm going to stop stealing, cursing, and cheating around with other men.

(Bridesmaid 2 looks up)

Please! Please! Jesus forgive me! I want to live for you!

Groomsmen 2 – Woman I've been doing everything under the sun including cheating on you too. I've been drinking my Busch beer and smoking my grass.

(groomsmen 2 falls to knees)

Please! Please! Jesus forgive me! I know my moma and daddy taught me good. I went to Sunday School , Vacation Bible School, Sunday Morning services and even night services too! Please! Please! Forgive me Jesus!

Jesus—In Acts 3:19-20 it says "Repent ye therefore and be converted, that your sins may be blotted out, when the times of refreshing shall come from the presence of the Lord; and he shall send Jesus Christ which before was preached unto you. Thou hast repented from thy sin, enter into the place I have prepared for you.

Bridesmaid 3 – I had a hard time this year. My husband lost his job. I am only working part time. The benevolence tried to help me out and even suggested that I should go get food stamps. You will never catch me in a line like that!

Groomsmen 3 – You are so right! We are church people. I'm the chairman of the Deacon Board. I'm the one they come to when they have a problem. They see me and not the pastor. When people look at me they don't see a weak man, they see a strong man.

Bridesmaid 3 – I know the pastor always says, 'We are saved by grace. But I don't sin, look at all the things I do in the church, I know I have God's favor!

Groomsmen 3 – Look at our walk . . . (bride and groomsmen walk with chest out)

Jesus – In Proverbs 16:18 it reads, "Pride goeth before destruction, and an haughty spirit before a fall." Pride tells you not to admit you are a sinner. Pride tells you, you are good enough to earn God's favor just the way you are. Pride has caused Satan to deceive you, just as he did Adam and Eve in the garden. Pride got in your way from loving and serving me. Depart from me you workers of iniquity.

(**Flower girl 1 and ring bearer 1 enters**)

Ring bearer 1 – We didn't obey our parents

Flower girl and ring bearer speaks together – repeating twice

Flower girl and ring bearer – Forgive us Jesus

Jesus—Colossians 3:20 reads, "Children obey your parents in all things for this is well pleasing unto the Lord." Since you have asked for forgiveness, I will give you a crown of life. Enter in the gates of Heaven.

Matron of Honor—Let me tell all of you some . . . . thing! Me! Myself! And I. I am the greatest singer in the church. Let me hit you a tune real quick.

(**Matron of honor sings Precious Lord**)

Matron of Honor – I just love to make the people shout, holler out, and run around like they are on a track, on my behalf, so I can get the credit. Well, let me go so I can get ready to sing in heaven. The angels can take notes on my voice and do what I do.

Jesus – You were given a gift that you can use along with God or with the saints of God. Yes, you have a glorious voice, but I didn't receive your praise! You only sing to impress people and didn't praise me. In Psalms 150:1-6 it say, "Praise ye the Lord, Praise God in his sanctuary; praise him in the firmament of his power. Praise him for his mighty acts, praise him according to his excellent greatness. Praise him with the sound of the trumpet, praise him with the psaltery and harp. Praise him with the timbrel and dance, praise him with stringed instruments and organs. Praise him upon the cymbals, praise him upon the high sounding cymbals. Let everything that hath breath praise the Lord, praise ye the Lord." And you didn't do none of that! Depart from me!

(Hell Bride entrance – Remain Silent)

Pastor: Jesus I put one of my members under the leadership of my Assistant Pastor. She should have received the teaching that would have kept her off the Streets. She was one of my best tithers. When she was on the mission program, the Lord would use her. She always arrive at church early, even before the deacons. Now I present the Church Bride to you.

Jesus: Ezekiel 3:17-19 says, "Son of man, I have made thee a watchman unto the house of Israel: therefore hear the word at my mouth, and give them warning from me, when I say unto the wicked, thou shalt surely die: And thou givest him not warning, nor speakest to warn the wicked from his wicked way, to save his life; the same wicked man shall die in his iniquity; but his blood will I require at thine hand. Yet if thou warn the wicked and he turn not from his wickedness, nor from his wicked way, he shall die in his iniquity; but thou has delivered thy soul." You should have been the watchman over her soul. You should have been Preaching Sound Doctrine and Living a Godly Life. Instead you preach to please the people and put your responsibility on others. Your main concern was watching how much they were giving in tithes, instead of watching for a change in their Life, So you and your member, shall live in Hell forever! Depart from me.

Intermission

(To give time for scene changes)

Continue reading for Scene Two

HEAVEN

(Introduction)

Who is the church?

The body of baptized believers known as the church are those that trust in Jesus Christ as their personal Savior.

Christ, the bridegroom has sacrificially and lovingly chosen the church to be his bride. Just as the bride and groom is separated from each other, so is the bride separated from her bridegroom, during the church age. The church bride's responsibility during the separation is to be faithful, to be a witness, to work in the church, and to love one another. Christ will return at an unknown hour and his people must be ready. Being ready means preparing for whatever contingency arises in our lives, keeping our eyes fixed on Jesus and being true worshippers for him.

As you will see, the church bride has been ready for a long time. She has been faithful, and obedient to the word of God. She has had her share of trials and troubles. She has prayed and fasted, waiting for her bridegroom, Christ to come. She then discovered that Christ was there all the time.

When Christ returns (the second coming) He's coming back for a church without a spot or wrinkle. The church bride will be arrayed in fine linens, which is the righteousness of the saints.

As believers of Christ Jesus, we who are the bride of Christ, wait with anticipation for the day when we unite with the bridegroom, our Lord and Savior Jesus Christ—to live with him eternally.

Characters

Bridesmaid 1, 2, 3

Groomsmen 1, 2, 3

Flower Girl

Ring Bearer

Heaven Bride

Scene II

Groomsmen 1: I'm sure we have made an impact on somebody's life.

Bridesmaid 1: Yes, the Lord used you on last Sunday and three came to Christ. In times like these, people want to hear a message that fit them or make them happy. They don't want to hear about homosexuality is an abomination to God. It was just a powerful message and it will draw you nearer to God. I thank God for the message and messenger. (Lift hands up in the air) Halleluah! Halleluah! Thank you! Thank you! Jesus!

Groomsmen 1: I heard you, teaching on forgiveness. If you don't forgive others, God can't forgive you! But you got a little deep when you were talking about the types of wounds. I like it when you said, a wound is a superficial cut. You can't see the cut; you can only feel the cut. In other words, sometimes this happens to us in our lives, we barely feel the pain and we brush it off and hope it gets better. I've heard a lot of teachers who have only skimmed the surface of this lesson, but when you get into the word and explain it to where a child can understand and relate it to their everyday lives. At that point they can begin to live the word.

Jesus Well done thou good and faithful servant; you have preached an uncompromising gospel and taught the truth. Enter thou into the joy of the Lord.

Bridesmaid 2: Let me tell you a little secret, those people at Redemption of Sin Church , they get on my last bar of soap! They always talking about Jesus but their actions show differently.

Groomsmen 2: Yeah . . . . like Sister Rockermore. She thinks she's the only one who can sing and the only song she knows is Jesus! Jesus! What a wonderful child, Jesus! Jesus! So sweet and mild. She sounds like me (can not sing)

Bridesmaid 2: Yeah . . . That's exactly right!

Groomsmen 2: I know I am right. They think that they are so saved and sanctified. They are weak minded, controlled by sin. They need to be more like us.

Bridesmaid 2: Yeah, we are not like they are. We don't gossip and I bet we can teach them something.

Groomsmen 2: We got it together! Let them lead each other in the hole. Come on!

Jesus: For I say through the grace given unto me, to every man that is among you, not to think of himself more highly than he ought to think; but to think soberly, according as God hath dealt to every man the measure if faith. Instead of seeing yourself and others as God see you, you evaluate yourself by the world standards. You see your worth as being more than others. Depart from me.

Maid of Honor: God has blessed me with the gift of praise dance. I know I have been anointed for this ministry. When I dance it moves people. They cry, they shout, and sometimes they even run. I'm just that good; people ask me from all over Houston to perform or teach their ministries about praise dance. I am just that good. When people lift you up you can get caught up in yourself and forget who brought you thus far. I had to fall down on my knees and ask God to forgive me.

Jesus : In I Corinthians 12:7 it says "The gift that you were given was intended for everyones benefit." It's when you serve others that your spiritual gifts emerge. God uses you to teach, encourage, and strengthen others. It was God and not you. God works through you. You may enter.

(Entrance of flower girl and ring bearer)

Flower girl and Ring Bearer: (singing) Jesus Loves Me!

Finale

(Entrance of the Church Bride)

Pastor: I present to you a faithful servant. One who is obedient to the word of God. One who has sacrificed her time, money, and talents. This is for the equipping of the saints for the work of the ministry, for the edifying of the body of Christ. The scriptures says if we live in the spirit, let us also walk in the spirit. We know that we are born in sin, shaped in iniquity. The spirit transforms our character whereby we can take on the fruit of the spirit. I present to you the church bride.

(Pastor gives the bride hand to Jesus)

Jesus: Matthew 25:21 says, "Well done, good and faithful servant; you were faithful over a few things, I will make you ruler over many things." Enter into the joy of your Lord.

Sister Annette Guillory–Wallace
Writer and Director

Annette Guilllory-Wallace is a writer, director, musician and song writer. She is a native of Houstonian. She is the daughter of the late Rev. and Sis. Carrean Guillory. Her family legacy entails a long line of talented musicians, singers and drummers.

In 2009, Sister Lee shared her inspirations for the play – "Be Careful What You Say (Watch Your Tongue)" and God went to work placing the words to paper. Annette Guillory has written Heaven's Gate and Hell's Fire which was performed by starlight Missionary Baptist Church Choir. She has written approximately ten songs such as "God Will Be There on Time", "Can't Stop, Won't Stop", and "I'll make It Somehow".

Annette Guillory – Wallace is currently the musician of the Starlight Missionary Baptist Church and the Praise Team president under the leadership of Rev. Allen T. Guillory Sr. The Lord has done wonderful things in her life. May God continue to bless all her endeavors.

BE CAREFUL WHAT YOU SAY
(WATCH YOUR TONGUE)
INTRODUCTION

The tongue is a powerful organ. It can speak life or cause death. The death can be physical, emotional, or spiritual. The bible says the tongue is as sharp as a sword. It can cut, maim, and destroy. The tongue can tear down or build up. With our tongues, we break spirits, we become stumbling blocks, and we can destroy relationships. The devil is accusing us to God, and is always trying to destroy our relationship with him. The good news is with our tongues, we can edify and encourage. People are healed by a word. Lazarus came back from the dead with words spoken by Jesus. Before we can be saved, we must confess with our mouths. Our number one communication with God is through prayer.

In this play, mankind has been found guilty, and has been sentenced to death. Mankind was born in sin and shaped in iniquity with a need to be saved. No matter how good we try to be, we can not save ourselves. The play is set at the execution of mankind. Normally at an execution, there is a variety of people who come to witness the event. Sometimes they are allowed to make a statement. The person sentenced to death is also given an opportunity to say one last thing. At the start of this play, the prosecutor, the warden and the executioner are talking. They are preparing to carry out the death of mankind. In this play, the warden is represented by sin. A warden also has custody or control over the condemned. Likewise, sin imprison, and prevents us from freedom. In that sin lays the power of death. The executioner, and death has the power of the grave, and that power condemned mankind to the grave. Satan takes on the role of the prosecutor. Satan uses all kinds of tricks to blind us before he tries to take us out. The bible declares that he is our adversary and he is like a roaring lion walking about seeking whom he may devour. He desires to sift us as wheat. The ten witnesses to the execution denote ten different types of tongues. Five are good and five are bad. Each one has contributed to making mankind what it is, and they want to tell you how. The play begins:

Characters:

Reporter Warden Prosecutor Executioner Camera Man Jesus A man

Crowd holding signs 2 Prison Guards

5 Bad tongues: Boastful Accusing Smooth Deceitful Malicious

5 Good Tongues: Wise Praying Instructed Righteous Rejoicing Jesus God

Be Careful What You Say
Watch Your Tongue!

(The warden is standing center stage; the prosecutor enter in from the side door)

Warden: Morning Mr. Prosecutor.

Prosecutor: Today is a good for an execution. Today mankind gets what's coming to him.

Warden: Yeah! You snagged him, and I'll bag him.

Prosecutor: And death will tag him. I worked hard to get mankind sentenced to death. I worked day and night collecting evidence on all mankind wrongdoings. Shoot, I even set some traps, some snare for mankind to get entangled in. It was real easy. Sometimes too easy! Mankind seemed to be looking for trouble. Even when mankind thought about doing the right thing, I was lurking at every corner. I had many others working for me. Making sure mankind fell over and over again. Ha! It worked and mankind was found guilty and sentenced to death. Yeah, today is a good day!

Warden: Then I got him! I made sure he was bound and shackled. I made sure that there was no escape. Mankind will never be free again thanks to us. You ought to see him. I bound his hands with fear. I bound his feet with doubt. I even used strong holds around his neck to muzzle him like an ox. After today mankind will be forever in darkness, never to see the light again!

(Prosecutor and warden give each other a high five with their hands as death enters)

Executioner: (speaks in a deep voice while turning to shake the prosecutor and warded hands) Satan, sin, everything is ready for mankind to die. I have been waiting for this day for a long time! Mankind is mine, and I will have him forever! Guards, bring in the prisoner!

Scene setting takes place outside of the prison. There is a crowd of people outside the prison. Some carry signs that read save mankind and others read man should die. There is a reporter present interviewing those who are attending the execution. Others attending are the tongues that either contributed to the guilty verdict or who tried to save mankind as a character witness.

Reporter: Good evening! This is Maria Rosalinda Juanita Gomez! I'm here at the Texas "everybody dies" State Prison, where their motto is," If you did it, then you're gonna get it!" There is a feeling of despair in the atmosphere. Mankind has been found guilty, and is scheduled to pay the ultimate price. This is the end of mankind! The fat lady has sung, and Elvis has left the building! Stay tuned as we give you a blow by blow account of today's events. I'm Maria Rosalinda Juanita Gomez, and we will be right back!

(reporter looks in camera)

Reporter: And cut! How was that!

Cameraman: Perfect!

Reporter: Quick get ready! Someone's coming!

(Reporter and cameraman run towards the 1ˢᵗ tongue)

I. The Deceitful Tongue

Reporter: Excuse me! Are you here for the execution of mankind? Deceitful tongue (dressed in drag) – Who me? No, I'm not!

Reporter: Really? Then why are you here?

Deceitful tongue: Who me? Oh I'm here for the execution of mankind!

Reporter: But that's what I asked you, and you said no!

Deceitful tongue: Who me? Oh child, don't mine me. I'm the lying tongue, you sees! But my friends call me deceitful!

Reporter: Well that explains a lot! So how are you mixed up in all of this?

(Reporter looks the deceitful tongue up and down)

Deceitful tongue: Who me? Well I played a big part in mankind demise! Do you remember when Jacob wanted his brother Esau's birthright? It didn't stop there you know. Jacob also wanted his blessings! But to do this, him and his mother, girl, they had to use me. Yes they did honey! Tricked the poor daddy with goatskin and good eating! They made it seem like Jacob was his brother Esau. Esau was a hunter and real hairy, but Jacob was smooth and stayed near the tent. Then Jacob used me to out right lie on God to his father's face. Oh I was very important in the demise of mankind.

Reporter: Well I have to agree with you! Thank you!

II. The Instructed Tongue

Reporter: I wonder who could be next. Was there no good to mankind?

Instructed tongue: I think I can answer that.

Reporter: And you are?

Instructed tongue: Instructed tongue!

Reporter: And you can tell my viewers some good about mankind.

Instructed tongue: No doubt. See God had a servant named Moses, and God had a job for him to do. He wanted him to deliver his people out of bondage. But Moses, being all man, wondered why anyone would listen to him especially a king. This is where I came into play. Although reluctant, Moses used me to tell the people and Pharoah just what God told him to. It took several instructions, but it seemed the king got the picture. Unfortunately, the Pharoah didn't heed the instructions. Pharoah lost his son and his army. God then gave Moses the ultimate instructions, the ten commandments. Moses used me again to instruct the Israelites what God himself imprinted in the stone. This is the main reason mankind is in trouble. He hated instruction, and for that reason he is a fool. Foolish is as foolish does. If mankind would just have listened to me! So sad!

Reporter: It seems so simple!

Instructed tongue: It is! Good day to you!

Reporter: Wow! I hope this is helping someone. I know I'm learning a lot.

III. The Accusing Tongue

Reporter: What was mankind thinking? How did I get to this point?

Accusing tongue: I think I can answer that. You did it!

Reporter: I did it?

Accusing tongue: Yeah! You, you, you and you did it!

Reporter: Why me?

Accusing tongue: Why not you! You think you're better than everyone else, don't you? I bet you started all of this!

Reporter: Why would you think that? Why are you accusing me?

Accusing tongue: it's what I am. It's who I am. I'm the accusing tongue.

Reporter: Whew! At first I thought you meant all that nonsense you were spewing.

Accusing tongue: It doesn't have to be true in order for me to accuse you. I could easily make up some stuff to blame on you, and people will believe it. I've done it before, and I can do it again.

Reporter: I s that so?

Accusing tongue: Yes that is so! Remember Jeremiah the prophet? You know the one that God said, "Before I formed thee in the belly I knew thee; and before thou camest forth out of the womb I sanctified thee, and I ordained thee a prophet unto the nations." Well, God sent him to tell the people that if they didn't turn from their evil ways and doings, that he would devise a plan that would be devastating. It would be so bad that people passing will shake their heads in astonishment. He said he would even turn his back on them, so whatever happens to them happens. And instead of listening to Jeremiah, they responded by using me and saying, "Let's attack him with our tongues and pay no attention to anything he says." They accused him of lying about what was going to happen. For that Jeremiah asked God to go ahead and punish them. For he tried to save them, and they accused him. Daniel was another one. Those in high office even created a decree just to accuse him of breaking it. He was sentenced to the lion's den, but God brought him through. So see the truth isn't necessary for me to do my job. And seeing that we are here today, I think I did it quite well!

Reporter: It seems that way.

Accusing tongue: No one ever accused you of being wrong! I am the man! See ya!

IV. Rejoicing Tongue

Reporter: Who could possibly be next? Do I hear singing?

Rejoicing tongue (enters singing) " Rejoice in the lord always and again I say rejoice! (or bringing in the sheves)

Reporter: Aren't you in a good mood!

Rejoicing tongue: (singing) Hallelujah! And why shouldn't I be?

Reporter: You do know today is the day that mankind dies? It's a very sad day.

Rejoicing tongue: Child, this is the day that the lord made. Let us rejoice and be glad in it! What has happened to mankind is very tragic, but God is still good!

Reporter: True! What is your name?

Rejoicing tongue: I am the rejoicing tongue (starts singing again)

Reporter: That you are! Mankind couldn't have possibly used you and still be in this predicament.

Rejoicing tongue: Oh I assure you he did. Using me was not mankind's problem!

Reporter: What was his problem then?

Rejoicing tongue: Forgetting why he used me in the first place.

Reporter: I don't follow you.

Rejoicing tongue: Let's use the children of Israel for example. They were slaves to Pharoah and his kingdom. They worked constantly with little or no reward. God sent his servant to free them, and he did. Yes, they were grateful and rejoiced for a little while. But when an obstacle came, they started complaining. At one point, they even started making golden images and worshipped them. This was a continual cycle. God would bless them, they would praise, they would forget and anger God and bring his wrath down on them. Then it would start all over again. And then there's King David. He was a man after God's own heart. He rejoiced right out of his clothes. He gave him an undignified praise for choosing him to lead the people. God blessed him and his home. He won battle after battle. Then he saw Batsheba naked, bathing from the rooftop, and lost his mind. He forgot all about God and using me to praise him. He knew she was married and still he slept with her while her husband was at war.

Reporter: Oh no!

Rejoicing tongue: It gets worst! After finding out she was pregnant, David sent for her husband. He tried twice to make him go homes and sleep with her so he would assume he was the father. When this didn't work, he had the husband sent to the front lines where he was killed. Oh sure, he felt remorse, and he used me to write a number of Psalms to God. He praised him, and urged others to do the same. The 103rd number of Psalms he wrote said, "Bless the lord, oh my soul and all that is within me, bless his holy name. Bless the lord, o my soul and forget not all his benefits. Some did, but most forgot why.

Reporter: Well, you keep doing what you're doing and maybe it can help mankind right now.

Rejoicing tongue: It's worth a try. God does inhabit the praise of his people (walks away singing)

Reporter: That he does!

V. Boastful Tongue

Reporter: Aren't you a colorful character?

Boastful tongue: Watch your tongue! No pun intended! I'm more than that. Can't you tell? Just look at me. (turns around)

Reporter: Let me guess, you're a gaudy tongue.

Boastful tongue: Excuse me!

Reporter: Tacky tongue, greedy tongue!

Boastful tongue: Let me stop you right there! I don't wanna brag, well I guess I do. I'm a boastful tongue!

Reporter: What do you have to boast about?

Boastful tongue: I helped kill one of the biggest men in the bible!

Reporter: And who would that be?

Boastful tongue: Goliiath of course! When he saw that David was sent to fight him, he was appauled and insulted. You see, David was only a boy, ruddy and handsome, and he despised him. He used me when he started with all the what am I a dog, that you come at me with sticks?" See usually anyone who intends to fight has on a coat of armor and a bronze helmet on his head, but David only came with five smooth stones and a sling shot. All Goliath saw was a small child, but he missed that God was with David. With all his boasting,

Goliath was killed with one stone straight to the forehead, and then was beheaded with his own sword. You know what the lord says, "Let not the wise man boast of his wisdom or the strong man boast of his strength or the rich man boast of his riches. Therfore, let no man think highly of himself more highly than he ought to think.

Reporter: Then where does that leave you?

Boastful tongue: Hold up, wait a minute! You right! I guess if mankind would have listened, I would exist, but he didn't, and I do exist. Bam! Check me out! (hums and speak low-"don't you wish your girlfriend was hot like me!) Toodles!

Reporter: How's that for news? Stay tune for the rest of the coverage of "mankind-the end"

VI. The Wise Tongue

Reporter: Thank you for tuning in to the second half of our report-"Mankind –The End." Someone's coming now. Let's see if they will talk to us! Hello! What do you know about today's events?

Wise tongue: Well, I'm smart enough to know that mankind would have used me more, none of us would be here today.

Reporter: That's a bold statement to make! Who might you be!

Wise tongue: When words are many, sin is not absent, but he who holds his tongue is wise

Reporter: Oooookkkay

Wise tongue: Reckless words pierce like a sword, but the tongue of the wise bring healing!

Reporter: Let me take a stab in the dark. You have to be the wise tongue.

Wise tongue: That is correct! Don't get me wrong. There have been many times mankind used me. Too bad it was not enough.

Reporter: We've heard a lot today. Mostly negative things were said. If you can give us a ray of sun in this otherwise cloudy day, please continue.

Wise tongue: Well there was a king that could have asked for anything in the world, but he chose me. He didn't want riches or honor. He wanted wisdom. He wanted to be able to discern right from wrong. For that reason, God gave King Solomon riches and honor along with wisdom.

Reporter: Did he do any good with the wisdom God gave him?

Wise tongue; Sure he did! Now two prostitutes came to the king. One of them said, "My lord, this woman and I live in the same house. I had a baby while she was there with me. The third day after my child was born, this woman also had a baby. During the night this woman son died because she laid on him. So, she got up in the middle of the night and took my son from my side while I, your servant was asleep. She put him by her breast and put her dead son by my breast. The other woman said, "No! the living one is my son, the dead one is yours!" And so they argued before the king. The king said, "Bring me a sword! And then he gave an order "Cut the living child in two and give half to one and half to the other". The woman whose son was alive was filled with compassion for her son and said to the king, "Please, my lord give her the living baby! Don't kill him!" But the other said, "Neither I nor you shall have him, cut him in two!" Then the king gave his ruling, "Give the living baby to the first woman, do not kill him; she is his mother. When the king's people heard this they were in awe because they knew that it came from God. Sad to say it didn't last.

Reporter: Maybe this great king could have helped mankind today. He needs someone on his side.

Wise tongue: Indeed!

VII. Smooth Tongue

Reporter: This execution is really bringing out everyone and they are spilling it all. Pardon me, what brings you here?

Smooth tongue: Oh I come to see my handy work first hand.

Reporter: Your handy work?

Smooth tongue: Yes I did more than my share in making mankind guilty. You're so beautiful and sophisticated! I love your look!

Reporter: (blushing) Oh how sweet of you to say! What were we talking about again? Oh yeah! What did you do?

Smooth tongue: Nothing big. I was just used to try and get Joseph into bed. You know the one who had the coat of many colors! You know he is sooo fine and good looking! The only problem was it was the wife of potiphar that was using me. She wanted Joseph so bad, but he refused her. She must have been butt ugly, I mean beautifully challenged, because he ran out of that house so fast he left his cloak. Feeling rejected she of course wanted revenge. This woman was slick and smooth. What better way to get revenge, but to use me the smoothest of them all. That's how I got my name.

Reporter: That would me?

Smooth tongue: Oh I'm a smooth tongue. Anyway, she screamed rape, and said he left his cloak when she began to yell. Her husband got so mad because of her lies, that he put Joseph in prison. Some people believe anything if it sounds good to the ear, no matter if it doesn't make sense! Well, I'll be on my way! Ta Ta mow!

Reporter: No wonder mankind is in trouble!

VIII. Righteous Tongue

Reporter: What a day this has been! There's been just a wealth of information. It's hard to take it all in. I can't wait to see what's next. Hello there!

Righteous tongue: Well hello! The day is almost over and the sun is going down,

Reporter: Yes that's true!

Righteous tongue: The time is right and the lord is just. What is to happen here today is both sad and unavoidable.

Reporter: Excuse me! Who are you?

Righteous tongue: I am the righteous tongue, but there is no me without him. There can only be righteousness through God. Mankind tried to be right. Mankind tried to be virtuous, but he failed time and time again. However, there was a few that God personally considered upright. Job was one of the few. He was blameless and he shunned evil and feared God. God believed in him so much that he offered Job as a test to Satan. Satan took Job's money and land, house and cattle, even his sons and daughters. Then Satan was allowed to smite him with boils. But does Job sin or curse God, no! instead he uses me to say, "Blessed be the name of the Lord! But of course everyone can't be righteous. His wife actually told him to curse God and die! But wait, there's more! His friends assumed that he was being punished because he had sinned. You know how people are! If there is any sign of trouble, they automatically assume you are being punished! But they should learn as Job did that God is sovereign. He'll do what he wants to whenever he wants to! Job questioned God, but acknowledged that God is the supreme ruler. God blessed Job with more than he had at first.

Reporter: We sure could use a righteous upright man today!

Righteous tongue: If God's willing, one will come!

IX. Malicious Tongue

Reporter: There are so many levels to mankind. I can't imagine what else there could be.

Malicious tongue: Who cares about mankind? Mankind deserves everything he gets.

Reporter: This is new. Who might you be?

Malicious tongue: I'm a malicious tongue, and I did everything I could to destroy mankind!

Reporter: Wow! Most of the other tongues I've spoken to, good or bad, has felt sorrow for mankind.

Malicious tongue: Well not me! I couldn't be happier! God knows I did my part to express man's hateful, spiteful, and vengeful ways.

Reporter: How pray tell?

Malicious tongue: The person that used me put an end to one of the greatest prophets who ever lived.

Joyce Lee

Reporter: Really! Tell us more!

Malicious tongue: See what had happened was King Herod married and laid with his brother's wife. He also put John the Baptist in prison for telling him that it is not lawful and you have no right to have your brother's wife. The wife heard about what John was saying and held a grudge against him, but she couldn't harm him. But an opportune time came (for Herodias) when Herod on his birthday gave a banquet, and her daughter performed a dance for him. It please and fascinated Herod to say the least.

Reporter: Oh so that's where it started! Did she have a pole too?

Malicious tongue: As I was saying before I was rudely interrupted. He was so happy, that he offered her whatever her heart desired.

Reporter: Yeah that's usually what comes next!

Malicious tongue: Anyway! The daughter ran to her mother to see what she should ask for, and her mother said the head of John the Baptist. The king was bound by his word and ordered John the Baptist's head on a platter.

Reporter: So that's where that phrase comes from! Man, that's real life Jerry Springer stuff! You definitely did your part!

Malicious tongue: That's what I said. I got to go, but don't think I forgot about your interruptions earlier. You better watch your back. In the shower, eating on picnics, you better watch your back.

Reporter: I see! (malicious tongue walks off) (reporter whispers) Did you get that? Just in case!

X. Praying Tongue

Reporter: Someone else is on the way! It looks as though their head is down and their eyes are closes, but they are walking straight towards us! (praying tongue stops right in front of the reporter) Excuse me! How are you doing that? Better yet why are you walking with your eyes closed?

Praying tongue: Just fulfilling my purpose! Thank you oh heavenly father!

Reporter: And what might that be?

Praying tongue: To pray without ceasing! Have mercy oh lord and lift mankind up from the gates of death. Have mercy O God according to your unfailing love, according to your great compassion, blot out my transgressions.

Reporter: Oh so you must be a praying tongue! (praying tongue nods head) Do you think that prayer will actually help mankind out of this tragedy?

Praying tongue: Don't know! All I can do is pray about it. God says in his word, I will have mercy on whom I will have mercy, and I will have compassion on whom I have compassion. It did work for some wayward people. For instance, it worked for Jonah. God had given Jonah a task, and he decided he was not going to do it. So he tried to run away and hide from God. Can you believe that? As if that's a possibility! He went on this boast, but the men figured out it was Jonah causing a violent storm that threatened to sink the ship. So, they threw him overboard, and he was swallowed by a whale. He stayed in that whale for three days and three nights. He used me to pray and repent to the lord, and the lord commanded the fish, and it vomited Jonah onto dry land. So , it worked for Jonah!

Reporter: Wow! So what should mankind do?

Praying tongue: Well the word says if my people, who are called by my name will humble themselves and pray and seek my face and turn from their wicked ways, then will I hear from heaven and will forgive their sin and will heal their land.

Reporter: Well maybe mankind will remember that!

Praying tongue: I'LL PRAY THAT HE WILL!

Reporter: So will I

XI. The Execution

Reporter: Well there you have it folks. It seems that the time has come to bid farewell to mankind. We will continue to bring you full coverage of the end of mankind. Let's go inside!

Executioner: Ladies and Gentlemen. We have come here to witness the execution of mankind. Mankind has been sentenced to death because of sin, and was unable to save himself. Before we put mankind to death, he may have a few minutes to speak. Mankind the floor is yours.

Mankind: Well I was born in sin and shaped in iniquity. From the beginning, I was hardheaded. I wouldn't listen to instruction. I would hear the word of the wise. Sure I rejoiced in victories, but I also rejoiced in the pain I caused others. I maimed and killed. I lied and deceived many. I did some good. Sometimes I fed the hungry, and gave water to those that were thirsty. But for all my good deeds, I was still sentenced to death. I'm sorry for the wrong I've done, and to all I've hurt. I don't want to die. I pray, please forgive me God!

Executioner: Ha ha ha! There's no one that can save you now. Not Moses or Daniel or Jeremiah. No one!

God: For I so loved the world, I gave my only begotten son in whom I am well pleased. That whosoever believeth in him shall not perish, but shall have everlasting life.

Jesus: I come that you might have life and have it more abundantly. I lay down my life, but pick it up again so that you may live. I give up my life so that you can have yours. I paid the ultimate price, so that mankind will be saved. I am freed from the agony of death, and death has no hold over me. Because of this, you are pardoned and have victory over Satan and death

Executioner: Noooooo!

Jesus: Where oh death is your sting?

(Satan, sin and death run away screaming) The chains are broken and mankind is free.

Mankind: (leaping for joy) I am free, thank you Jesus.

Jesus: Go ye therefore and teach all nations, baptizing them in the name of the father, in the name of the son, and in the name of the Holy Ghost.

Mankind: (walks down the aisle singing) I am free praise the lord I'm free.

Voice of God: (Person with microphone – not seen) We were all sentenced to death under the law. If we sin, we would certainly die. For indeed, the wages of sin is death, but hallelujah, the gift of God through Jesus is eternal life. When we accept Jesus we are saved from eternal damnation. We have the ability to put Satan under our feet. We have the capability to say to the mountain be thy removed. We can speak the name of Jesus and make demons tremble. We all fit one or more of the tongues that was represented in this play. We all have a choice to speak life or speak death. Either way, we will have to deal with the consequences. Be careful what you say!

Scripture References

Deceitful tongue Psalms 50:19

Instructed tongue Psalms 32:8

Accusing tongue St. Luke 11:54

Rejoicing tongue Philippians 4:4

Boastful tongue Psalms 94:4

Wise tongue Proverbs 15:2

Smooth tongue Proverbs 6:24

Righteous tongue Psalms 37:30

Malicious tongue 3 John 1:10

Praying tongue James 5:16

CPSIA information can be obtained at www.ICGtesting.com
Printed in the USA
LVOW131445250512

283343LV00010B/123/P